The Fly in My Eye

The Fly in My Eye

Musings of Mind and Spirit

J. MICHAELS

RESOURCE *Publications* · Eugene, Oregon

THE FLY IN MY EYE
Musings of Mind and Spirit

Resource Publications
An Imprint of Wipf and Stock Publishers
199 W. 8th Ave., Suite 3
Eugene, OR 97401

www.wipfandstock.com

ISBN 13: 978-1-60899-935-4

Manufactured in the U.S.A.

*To all my friends and family
who still can't figure out just what the hell
I'm doing working as a poet*

Contents

Preface

IMPUNITY IS DEFINED AS *freedom from unpleasant consequences*. If that is truly the case, then we all must live lives of unconscious impunity. By that I mean although we continually experience the consequences of the material life, we do so without being aware of the source of many of those consequences. We are then left to our own devices to try to understand the true causes of seemingly random effects. This is the proverbial *blind spot* inherent within the narrow confines of the human perceptual experience.

We seem to be at the mercy of the world and all of its myriad and random occurrences: *An earthquake includes us and we are its victim due to its seeming enormity and invincibility. A friend turns on us for no apparent reason and we are left to choose between blaming and rationalization.* And although we spend an inordinate amount of time trying to control our lives and those in our care, we all know in the recesses of our mind that control is simply not possible in such a world, and it scares the crap out of us! Yet we cling to this vast uncertainty and continue to expect it to improve. But we know it won't. It hasn't for centuries and the same old uncertainty continues to rule the world. So we turn our hope to fantasies in an attempt to live better in that delusion, even though we know that eventually it will turn on us as well, one day fatally.

It is quite ironic that we spend so much time indulging in fantasy (TV, video games, movies, pornography, nocturnal dreams, obsessions, wishes, etc.) but we are unable to accept the notion that the one remaining layer of our "reality" may be fantasy as well. If we are 90% immersed in dreams and fantasy, could we not be just as easily 100% immersed? The main tool of recognition in the material world is perception and it always represents as a subjective stance. Each *seeming* individual perceives the same time, space, object, subject, or situation differently, primarily based on their own perceptual filters culled from a limited knowledge and perspective. Is this not fantasy as well?"

So along comes this old guy who tries to tell you that this entire world may be a dream and you respond with, *what the hell is he talking about*? What I speak of is the notion that our so-called waking state is simply another level of dreaming and behind that final layer of fantasy lies a reality based on the truth. I, like you, have but two real choices; believe in the validity of this world with all its uncertainty, contradiction, absurdities, violence, and discord or allow my mind to accept the possibility that another, better reality exists. The only *better* reality I know of is the one conceived of by our divine Creator. Many of us, although the form does vary, believe in a Supreme Being who has done just that, yet we relegate that notion to the backrooms of our mind, residing very closely to our belief in other *nice to have* things.

One of the attributes of an omnipotent Creator is an all-knowing nature and that implies a single unified Mind. Few would argue that such a Creator would make as big a mess of things as we see in the material world. So if the Creator's Creation is a better reality and we are all, as Children of God, present in that single, unified Mind, is it not conceivable that the totality of the perceptual world is one big illusion? An illusion, dream, or fantasy made and maintained by the sleeping part of the one Mind? How else do we reconcile our inherent divine nature as children of God with the treatment we receive as humans? Is God vindictive? Cannot He handle the job? Are these questions any less absurd than the notion that this perceptual world is not His, but rather our own limited mental invention?

I realize the enormity of trying to convince anyone of the fallacy of a life whose validity is continually reinforced by a constant barrage of sensory data. Yet we all know intuitively that life is composed of much more than sensory input. If it were not, we would fail to experience the most precious of life's gifts; namely love, joy, peace, freedom and completion or fulfillment. But if you deem yourself ready to explore the possibility of a divine reality created by God and further to follow a path of potentialities engendered by that choice, I stand ready to lend a hand. I am a much simplified man, lately ridden of frail beliefs and notions that confine me to only the accepted forms of reality. I have seen, with my own inner connection to that one Mind, many wonderful aspects of the divine world. Yet I cannot convince you by means of sight or sound or feel, but only by the certainty you will experience upon encountering the same truth that has graced my life.

I have come to recognize *the fly in my eye;* that reflection left by my own projection and perceptual delusion. That picture of me and my world is simply what I have shown myself to be true. A picture painted by a small, sleeping part of my mind, an errant thought if you will, that I allowed to deceive me for want of a "better reality". Remove the fly from your eye, if you deem it timely, and together we will explore those other, better possibilities.

Think Me Christ

Do you think me Christ
Of course it is true
I am your only savior
And you are mine too

For God begat only one Son
We are but pieces of the Whole
Each containing the divine spark
That emanates from our soul

So think me Christ
Give me my holy due
And see yourself the same
Christ is both me and you

Receiving Hands

Who will get this book
Who will love its lines
Who will walk right into it
Who will their mind redefine

If it is meant for you, brother
Than I am happy bound
It means your time has arrived at last
The time for your soul to be found

So, who will get this book
I'm still not sure I know
I think it lands where it's supposed to
The receiving hands will know

The Fly in My Eye

What's gone awry
What's gone awry
What's gone awry
I've got something in my eye
Don't move, I'll get it
It might be a lonely fly
That sits upon my eye
Don't squish him, we're buddies
Though of different species we abide
I've grown accustomed to his loneliness
And he, to the fly in my eye

Into You

I can't get my mind around it
How can that be
Perhaps we are all mistaken
And the Mind is wrapped around me
To let go would be divine
It would likely set me free
Hold on, my Father, I'm coming
Into You is where I'll be

Broken Truce

Mim and Mip
Two twin sisters at three
Not too long after
They sat upon daddy's knee

One came away unscathed
The other, scarred for life
One in tenuous denial
The other in constant strife

They came of age anyway
Soon became some man's wife
And sat their child on daddy's lap
And brought their guilt to life
Staring accusingly at a good man's face
Seeing it away from light

Projecting now the guilt they owned
Upon a gentle man's brow
Depriving their children of trust
In the man that brought them about

Now all suffer and break
Never seeing their brother in truth
Apart and shattered they remain
With trust the broken truce

Boggled and Blown

I'm all boggled and blown
I seem to have lost some littleness
Giving up a mind of my own

A Place to Stay

It's a declining world
Providing less of what I see
An opening becoming smaller
Until finally I can be
In the company of my dear Father
With eyes that truly see

Witness to all around me
At last, arrived at Home
With nothing but peephole to see
The illusion we were loaned

I long for pure sight to arrive
And watch the world go away
Replaced by Paradise, my friend
Somewhere we all can stay

Prince of the Kingdom

Guru or gargoyle
What is your role to be
Which guise will you don
Which confusion will you see

Your life may run a varied track
It may take you where you please
Yet the only place it cannot take you
Is a home where all are free

It's a trap door of sorts
A contract to never see
While blindly playing a role
That defines who we be

It is but costume and dress
It knows nothing of who we are
We have but one true identity
The Prince of the Kingdom we are

Early Aplomb

Who would've thunk it
Holy words coming through me
Back in the day, all would doubt it
They would say, *how silly can you be*

For I was a bit of a bad boy
I wavered beyond the line
I got in a bit of trouble
I strayed from time to time

Yet everything seems to be forgiven
I become clearer every day
And start to see the reasons
Why I was chosen to be this way

I sit with some damn fine company
My new pals are quite the bomb
I'm so pleased with where I landed
Despite all the early aplomb

The Only Real Sin

A most commonsense creature
That *fly in my eye*
He cut me the thinnest slice
Of some lovely diet pie

He recited me some verse
From a previous attempt at such
He demanded my recognition
And required a tender touch

He said, *get off your duff now*
It's time to reel it in
Get your mind back to the basics
Lack of love is the only real sin

Medium Guy

I'm a medium guy
I tend to avoid extremes
I like to land in the middle
Only in the gentlest of streams
Only in the sweetest of dreams

Composed of average size
A *middle of the road* kind of guy
Until I beheld my Savior
And He welcomed me to the sky

He advised I would need to stray
From that line in the middle of the road
And get myself overloaded
With new ideas in a different mode
Rearrange my way of thinking
To accept the road as my own

A Place Called Home

This is what home feels like
Feet up at journey's end
Warm and safe and eternal
Among the best of friends
A glass of wine so fine
You can taste by smell alone
A morsel of cake so delicious
It attracts by sight alone
This must be the place they call home

Part of the Fun

It's part of the mystery
It's part of the fun
To instill multiple meanings
That take off and run
Through the chambers of our minds
To the very heart of our souls
Let these sane words carry us
To the love that unites the Whole

Love in Any Land

I would like to say it simply
For a simple man I am
Using the popular vernacular
I love those green eggs and ham

I am a grandpa in love, you see
With this precious light in my life
She teams up with my other love
Pairing with beloved wife

I am a man late of years
Having battled a host of fears
To come to the point of presence
Beyond the valley of tears

I say to you, my brother
That the key is in my hand
I give it freely to you
It's called love in any land

Treasure House Within

I'm jiggy with it
It comes as no surprise
I've handed it over to better hands
Bequeathed my vision to clearer eyes

I no longer make the rules
I defer to a higher court
Turned it over to my main man
And waited for his retort

Signing up with the good hands people
Requesting to know the way
Attentive and open to the answer
Am I leaving or do I stay

Either way, I'm primed for listening
My eyes as sharp as pins
Mind open to all bequeathed me
The treasure house within

Slightly Askew

Slightly askew
That was you
A square peg
In a very round hole
Too good for the world
And never a fit
Singing in the shower
Nary a note you ever hit
With a smile that ever lit
A troubled life for sure
But yet your heart was pure
The pain so hidden but not
So hidden you ever forgot
We all made a lot of mistakes
We didn't know what to do
But since I lost you, my son
My heart was cleft in two
Yet your worldly death did show me
A spiritual thing or two
It taught me sweet forgiveness
And that we're never through
For we live as one together
Then, now, and forever

(Chris, a poem slightly askew, in honor of you)

Ode to a Marriage

We've been through so much together
We've had a trial or two
Yet together we have remained
Proving our love was true

We have transcended man and wife
Becoming more than we two
We have learned to truly love
From God we take our cues

Our union has given immaculate birth
To this sweet child we both love
It has brought us peace so holy
Surely touched by God above

So I say to you, my sweet sister
That truly we have been blessed
Our lives now bound eternal
When in Heaven, we take our rest

No One to Blame

I am more informed now
Of the truth of the matter
I see the ego in its nakedness
I see now that it hardly matters

The cycle becomes clearer
Seeing the path of guilt
How it leads to my own punishment
And how my touch is felt

Attacking a brother for naught
Believing he deserved the pain
When in truth, he is me
And I am the one to blame

So I bestow upon myself
All pain, disease, then death
For I have clearly sinned
And cast a faulty breath

I become less with added attack
Except for my store of guilt
And continue to put upon my brothers
The unworthiness so very long felt

Together, we live in this world
Made of our guilt and shame
But take heart, my dearest brother
None of us are to blame

The Direction I Go

I deny now
What I know to be untrue
No longer will it linger
And tell me what to do

For the ego and its minions
Have nothing better to do
Than shed guilt and pain and torture
No matter what we do

It's all a lie, my brother
Something bought a long time ago
A package of non-delivery
A mechanism meant to slow

I will no longer heed
The loveless ego or its call
I choose my own direction
I choose the endless All

A Lesson Learned From Pizza

A lesson learned from pizza
That guilt is not my friend
I have eaten them both
And digested them within
Resulting in something quite odious
This fat and faulty frame
Having had the pizza for breakfast
Followed by desert, in shame
Crap them both out
We are deserving of a finer plate
We deserve no guilt of pizza
Or anything else that dims our fate
For we are true and holy
We are more than we even know
We have no need of pizza
Or the guilt that attaches it so

Toll to Pay

It's an odd day
It feels a bit out of kilter
I'm feeling a very strange way
Likely, it's a clogged up filter
That lights me up this day
I have learned a valuable lesson
In an unlikely and bizarre sort of way
I pray it's all over now
Leaving no toll to pay

Decisions

I shed my shoulds
Took another look
At what I could
Decided where I stood
And what may come through me
What should prevail
Decided what I wanted
What would succeed
And what would fail
I decided on God
The ego declined
But to no avail
I'm going home, my friend
Why not join me along the way
Make a decision
Sit down and pray
Find us all a better way
Make this your holiest day

In Between World

I'm in the between world
Neither here nor there
I'm here in the between world
I have no idea where

It doesn't feel like home
Nor an alien touch conveyed
It just feels like I'm nowhere
And there's little I can say

I know I've moved a notch
Yet little direction gives the day
I'm back to blind faith again
With little else to say

I tread unreported ground
I trust my Father to protect me
Regardless of where I'm found

Mysteries to resolve and say
The words I require of necessity
To tell me which way to pray

Endless Rhyme

I am unashamedly lyrical
I love a tidy rhyme
To hell with poetic convention
Let it stay in bounded time

The rhythm of the universe
May be wed to lovely words
The Song of Heaven may be sung
For all the angels to be heard

So allow me my rhyme
Let in dance upon my mind
Let it give me lovely willies
As it travels up my spine
For when it leaves the body
It will point to an endless time

He Was There

I've been to some of the foulest
Places you will ever see
I've indulged in back breaking pleasure
Going as deep as I could be

I've visited some dark places
They always took me in
Some almost swallowed me
And left me at my end

Yet someone was there
He was always there
Right before the grand flush
He showed me He was there

I knew I had never deserted
Nor He, the same, to me
Since time immemorial
I knew right then
He would always be

The Source

Much like a river flowing
Born of love surrounding
Like a breeze gently blowing
Stemming from a grounding
In a mystical sort of being
It doesn't stop and it's okay by me
It feeds and quenches my soul
It comes from source unending
From the eternal boundless Whole

Dismal Room

Chipping away at the illusion
This is what I do
Taking shots at what deludes us
Poking a hole to see through

For on the other side of nowhere
Is a place to be much desired
So much more than this locale
Of which I have become most tired

It waits for us now, my brother
Eternity in full glorious bloom
Release your investment in nothing
Let us leave this dismal room

The World We Bought

I followed an errant thought
It is what got me here
One slight departure from truth
That blinded the Heavenly sphere
A glimmer that caught my eye
Temptation of the fleeting kind
A mis-thought that bore no relevance
To the integrity of my mind
Yet I followed it anyway
I strayed from my sweet Home
Became lost in the illusion
Of having found a mind of my own
I see now the outcome
Of a loveless form of thought
It screams and lashes out at us
In this world of form we bought

Words That Touch Them True

I see the brilliance of them
These odes that touch my soul
I know from whence they came
Born of spiritual gold

I know not who will see them
In the light that graces my mind
They may fall on deafened ears
And eyes that remain as blind

It matters not how many
Only that it finds the few
Dear souls who await the delivery
Of words that touch them true

Only Love

At some depth within
The love of our Father dwells
At some level of deception
We cover it with dreams beheld

We want our place in Heaven
Whilst keeping a foot in place
We want to be forgiven
Yet still run the human race

Our soul cries out for union
With brothers one and all
Yet we keep our separate ways
Lest we trip, as humans, and fall

We abide our faith in Jesus
We pray both night and day
Yet we continue to worship the dollar
We still need our worldly pay

We will stride this line forever
As long as we continue as such
The difference between Christ and us
Is that, to Him, only love is us

Say of Me

If you can say of me
When I finally go
That a gentle man walked here
And left a bit of gold
Then I shall depart in joy
Back to my Father's Fold

A Place to Start

I have invited love in
And kicked fear out
Opening up to truth
Looking for a wisdom rout/e

For truth wears love's garb
Revealed beneath its wings
Enveloped in the words
That encourages my heart to sing

I am ready to be complete
Dissolving the egg of illusion
Revealing the magnificence replete
With beauty unimaginable
With love that will warm your heart
Join me brother in the sharing
What a wonderful place to start

Gone Fishin

Gone fishin, gone fishin, gone bye
Let's keep that deadly hook
From snagging on my eye
It could ruin the trip of fishin
Could certainly darken the way
Eyeing the collective fish
And releasing the catch of the day

(Now that, my friends, is a case of intentional ambiguity; perhaps)

Lovely Point of View

I claim sanity
I possess a clearer view
Seeing through the illusion
All the way to the heart of you
God has graced my sight
With a lovely point of view

The Race

Mr. and Mrs. Mucous
Have recently entered the race
They've found the world to be
A very slippery place

The track is getting soggy
Making it hard to run in place
The couple is beginning to doubt
The validity of the race

The clock is ticking faster
Trying to escalate the pace
Doubt is increasing as well
Challenging the veracity of the race

It's all adding up
To a substantial moral case
The dilemma will not be solved
By the running of the race

Christ is My Muse

Christ is my muse
There is no one else around
Questions and answers are posed
Solutions waiting to be found

At times, I think He's left me
My darkness does not invite
Yet I know He is with me forever
Never eluding my sight

Yet I remain blind in some respects
I lose sight from time to time
And then He appears within me
To remind me of our rhyme

It is the bond that keeps us
Within each other's view
He asks me to consider
Doing the same for you

Good Guys and Bad Guys

Round and round we go
Playing the game
Of good guys and bad guys
Needing someone to blame

A target for hate and admiration
Someone to take the fall
Someone to declare as winner
Someone to lose it all

A cast of characters well played
Toasting projections well laid
Some receiving our accolades
Some to reflect our fate

They all are born of mind
With ego pulling the strings
Good guys and bad guys
All born of love restrained

A Tighter Helm

Good afternoon
May I introduce a character or two
These are my good friends
Mr. and Mrs. Mucous and their two
This is Mr. and Mrs. Mucous' daughter Mim
Over there is the other clue
The daughter named Mip, here too
Quite a gathering we have here
The Mucous' and their brood
Sorting out the Mucous'
Could require a retooled attitude
So, to hell with it
Let's move on to broader realms
Let the Mucous fend for itself
We're taking a tighter helm

Via Electrons

It's a new age of communication
Coming alive in various form
Consummated and enlivened
Through channels that elude the norm

A rising of consciousness
Bubbling to the top
Disseminated via electrons
And giving the message some pop

It's Facebook, MySpace, and more
Lots of room to open those doors
Sending fair thoughts on airwaves
Knocking on King Cyber's door

It's tweeter your Twitter, or else
Or Twitter my tweeter, the rave
Don't forget to secure and encrypt it
Don't become its slovenly slave

Shit Storm

This writing I do
That comes from my heart
The words from Christ Divine
Of which I now take part

I assume they will kick up some dust
They will likely start a fight
It will probably be a shit storm
Of which I avoid in light

I do not intend to offend
I have no desire to start
This or any other storm
That distracts from words of the heart

I write that directed to write
I concur in my soul of souls
I will stand beside them
No matter how the storm unfolds

Old Fart

I'm an old fart
What can I say
I get to wear plaid
And say what I pray

The restraints are mostly gone
I have no one left to impress
I could walk down the street half naked
In case I forgot to get dressed

No one will likely care
Nor take a second glance
I'm too old to be considered
With or without my pants

But I'll tell you one thing
That you likely never thought
I have a bit of a treasure
Something that can't be bought

It's wisdom born of trouble
Experience at high paid price
I've learned to ignore this world
In favor of Heavenly Spice

So listen up, if you want to
Pay attention, if you have the time
I'll whisper a bit of it to you
But you'll have to keep up with the rhyme

It's my current way of conveying
The lessons I've learned to date
If you want the wisdom within
You'll just have to stay or wait

But have no fear, my brother
Your time will come at last
The words will come reach you
And remove you from your past
They will bring you Home forever
And offer you divine repast

An Old Fashioned Shellacking

Shaking things up
The gift from me to you
It's what's been granted
To show us what to do

Though we are but fairly lost
We have brothers who hold us fast
Connected as one, we are
A bond to eternally last

So hang on, it might get bumpy
We might hit a snag or two
We might run into each other
Not knowing what to do

Yet I say to you, my brother
I have friends in higher spheres
They are your friends as well
Faces washed by similar tears

We're shaking and baking as buddies
Overturning all that is false
Kicking up some dust in the process
Knocking down stalls and walls

I say we fasten our seat belts
Strap in and enjoy the ride
Let's see what gets overturned
What ends up on our side

We may find out very soon
That what we wanted was lacking
Perhaps what was needed all along
Was a good old fashioned shellacking

Just in Case

Don't eat that slice of pizza
Put down the cookies in hand
Step away from those biscuits
You're a bad, bad man

Don't you know you'll clog your arteries
Drive your blood pressure through the roof
You'll likely start up a new disease
Something like mouth and hoof

So stop right now, you glutton
Get on that treadmill instead
Wipe the butter off your face
Get up and out of that bed

You better turn over a new one
A livelier attitude will help
I want you to stop enjoying
Anything about yourself

Thin down and firm up
Or soon you'll need a tuck
Clean out those failing arteries
In case someone gives a fuck

The Voodoo We Sell

You do your voodoo
I'll turn a trick or two
Explain the voodoo you do
And we'll see what's left to do

A rabbit ejected from the hat
That he'd just grown accustomed to
Likely a bite on the butt
From trick in line number two

I think it's quite simple really
This voodoo we both do so well
It's nothing short of a miracle
That looks like the voodoo we sell

All He Asked of Fame

I will miss you George Carlin
You, of captivating wit
A shaker and mover of elite class
You came and shook things up a bit

Brandishing those twin six shooters
You came with guns a blazing
Letting us have it with both barrels
Leaving no doubt, you were amazing

What a mind, what a man
He challenged the ordinary way
He taught us to look at everything
In a discerning sort of way

Be not fooled, he would say
By the flagrant, flatulent, or profane
Suck it up and think about it
Was all he asked of fame

Friendly Flowers

A kindred soul goes down
No longer by me to stay
I've lost another companion
My life's a lonelier day

Yet keep hold my hand, dear brother
Let us stay as one friend this day
Fleeing the friendly flowers
As souls do dash away

We'll hang on, if you'd like to
Or we can simply say, *adieu*
We'll meet up on the other side
Friends reborn and renewed

Better Than Getting Laid

I've been asked about my persona
The image I put forth
I think it's a lively combo
Of Dylan and Carlin reborn
I've long been a fan of Bobbie's
He and I were woefully made
I love the sound of poetry
From ironic lips portrayed
Making me laugh and think about it
Was better than getting laid

No More Boners

The last poem posed the question
Is there anything better than getting laid
I'm not sure I answered it the first time
It's based on how little I get paid
When I count my blessings in orgasms
And how often I'm getting laid
So the answer to you, my friend
Is something to consider anew
What will you do with *Willie*
When all his boners are through

(I'll use him as garden hose, that is what I'll do)

Oceans Boat Denote

I swim uncharted waters
Trying to stay afloat
Holding to vessel supplied
It becomes my life support boat

Yet I know it is but fading
From sight and daily need
Preparing to submerge my being
In the Ocean where I feed

The oneness that obviates my boat
The oneness that crosses the moat
Letting go of said vessel
Letting waves bring me afloat
To land upon shores most inviting
A place which oceans denote

Woof Woof

Hoofs on the roof
Hoofs on the roof
I'm dancing a jig
On the top of my spoof
I dare you to stand there
And remain aloof
It's hard to deny that noise
When it's raising your roof
Woof, woof

(Intentionally ambiguous again? I don't think so)

Christ Mine

If this be the Christ Mind
Then hurry and sign me up
I can't wait to be a member
I can't wait to drink from that cup

Wonderful ideas abide there
Light dances with love as guest
A gift to all entitled
To illuminate the holy quest

It is our inheritance, my brother
It is the gift divine
Bestowed by a loving Father
It is both yours and mine

Free

I proceed unafraid
Love has joined me
Fear has left me
I am free

Guilt Trip

Every ache, every pain
Is a guilt pill
Embedded within your mind
It identifies as sin still
Yet it is but an illusion
A charade to take our attention
And move it from Heaven to hell
Yet we may love it all away
And teach our minds to tell
Of only purity and innocence
Tell the guilt to go to hell

Never Ending

Love never ends
Truth never ends
Peace never ends
Eternity never ends
God never ends
Where do you end

I end with God
Then never end

Out the Door

I think I'll order that biscuit today
I'll order it up without guilt
I'll take it with lots of butter
Adding extra bacon to the melt
For today I deny guilt
Its previous authorized way
I've decided to kick its ass
Out my door and make it stay

Faulty Body

I must be guilty
My body tells me so
It's obvious how fat I am
Ugly too, don't you know
Way too tall, fat, and wide
Just a tiny pest with nowhere to hide
I'm way too black or brown
I stutter and stammer incessantly
I have way too many anxieties
I hope my parents don't come to town
Well ……...
I'm here to tell you, brother
That it's all a crock of shit
I'm here to tell you, brother
The guilt just doesn't fit
A soul born into Christhood
By a perfect Father Who created it

Leaving

Do we truly believe our Father
Would leave us in the fray
You'll have to first convince me
There was no other way
Yet heed while I pose this question
That will speak to your very soul
How do we leave *Everything*
This is the riddle told

Tuning the Divine

Where do we turn our tuners
How do we know what to find
How do we acquire those existential stations
Where do we land in mind
Wherever our heart will take us
With God attuning the divine

Crazy and Loving It

This joy that attends me now
Feels a bit crazy at times
Yet I know it is realer than real
I'll make sweet insanity mine
For if this is whacked
Then I surely don't care
If anyone thinks I'm crazy
I'll tell them to stick it where
The sun don't shine, my darlin
And watch me not give a care

Colorado Land

Blue Colorado skies
Blanket of white adorn
Magnificent Rockies before me
It looks like Heaven's form

It is the lovely place I abide
It's my home away from Home
Yet I relish my time upon it
It remains the place I roam

I travel it from valley to peak
I absorb it in my soul
Colorado is part of me
My life has little foretold

I will take it with me when I leave
Its sweet spirit will honor my hand
Trading it in for Heaven
Paradise to be my new land

Second Look

Don't go all *Full Monty* on me
I don't wish to see your parts
I certainly am much more interested
In what abides your heart

There was a day I fancied parts
That time is nearly gone
I traded my bug eyes in
For a shot at atonement done

I'll need to break it to you sometime
There will be a need to speak up
Those parts may soon depart you
Leaving but an empty cup

So attach yourself, my brother
To the soul that rides the train
All the way to Paradise
Singing sweet Heaven's refrain

Tis hardly a trade worth mentioning
It's a deal in anyone's book
Lay down that diminishing body
Give your heart a second look

The Versifier

I found a new word upon searching
For a better way to say
That I'm in this for the long haul
I know of no better way

My new job is to be your scribe
Deliver what I've been told
The new word we just talked about
Will come from the rhymester, I'm told

It's merely another way to state
That my poems are here to stay
Versed by the versifier
Or portrayed by poet this day

Captain of the Trumpets

My Captain, my Captain
It is beyond me to say
How much love is in my heart
More than sweet words can say
I have found a home in You
Now forever Heaven bound
You are my royal Captain
I await command and sound
Of the trumpets of Paradise
Issuing that Heavenly sound

The Same Muse

The source of all genius
Comes from the same Muse
It is but for all of us
To accept, love, and use
All within the same Muse

What is Your Future

What is your future
This is what I say
Look not to tomorrow
It will be as it is today
If you live in the past
That will be your future
If you live but in the present
That will be your true life
This is what I say
But if you live in the future
You will never live in today

The Nearest Unbiased Wall

This is fun to do
I hope it is for you too
I like the skipping around
From one convention to the next
Playing with every other syllable
Rearranging and arranging the text

You must know by now
That I can't be trusted as such
To bring you the long expected
Or give credence to the normal so much

I will instead be guided
By the love that flows through my veins
And let it arrive as it wants to
I may write in a humorous vein

But either way, you'll get it
The juggling tools will fall
The answer will lay spelled out
On the nearest unbiased wall

See in a Simple Way

Symbols aren't nearly as satisfying
As the organic, homegrown thing
A word is only a word
Until it becomes a unified thing

What lies within that picture
Moving, still, or otherwise
Is still only a picture
It can't release or provide you wise
It will likely do the other
And induce an abundance of lies

Look beyond the celluloid paper
Peer through illusion's wall
Go beyond the plain and ordinary
To wisdom's door and stall
There to await instructions
And a Guide to show the way
We don't need no stinkin badges
Symbols will shrink this day
Leaving but truth to amaze
And welcome us, at last, to Heaven
Where we see in a simple way

An Entirely New Man

I think I created an opening
When I dropped my bag of crap
When I let the air out of ego
Started following a whole new map
It has led me to this sweet spot
Where love has taken a stand
It has opened and invited me in
Made me an entirely new man

Traveling a Foreign Land

From the hawk to the dove
I have traded for better wings
I have taken to fairer winds
Looking for finer things

I will speak love to you only
Let it grace your inner ear
I will show only oneness to you
Let it dissipate your fear

For I have only love to offer
Eternal life, its one true pal
Endless time graced with peace
With no checkout from this hotel

We will enter the Master's Chambers
He will lay touch with gentle hand
He will show us all we missed
While traveling in a foreign land

No Doubt

I have no doubt now
This is my only cue
I have but left one purpose
It is to bring love to you
The vehicle is obvious and true
I'll live as long as it comes through
Nothing else matters now
The love includes us all
I have no doubt I'll be here
Until I leave and that is all

New Me

I hope my friends can hear me
My family renews their hope
I am now this different person
Riding a slippery slope
It's much too grand to slow it down
You'll just have to wait and see
What continues to issue forth
From this new and adventurous me

Smaller Vices

Smaller vices pursue me now
Delights of a different sort
Not the ones that used to trap me
Of those I have little to report
Mine are stolen moments
The kind that come gently by
Staying just long enough
To stare me in the eye
And say to me, *see what's been missing*
From a life lived as blind
This is what's been missing
Of this, I've been most blind
God has been looking intently
And I have left Him behind
Now I see what I'm missing
I know of my Heavenly find

A Good Posture

I feel like I'm writing a weird bible
A tome of a different sort
It's all bundled up in rhymery
Giving forth the occasional retort
I don't know what to call it
I haven't the faintest clue
Let's just assume a good posture
Share it between me and you

Need to Know Basis

A while ago, I placed a bet
On a most comely come or go
I ventured that love would attend me
Possibly in a month or so

Per truth, I never knew
And perhaps should have never said
But I sure as hell had my hopes up
To taste that Heavenly Bread

Well guess what, people
I've finally made the grade
Love has come to visit
And take me beyond the grave

I'm not certain of that time either
Some things are better unknown
I have faith the utmost in my Beloved
He will grant me as I need to know

Friends From Afar

He's a California boy
I'm a Colorado guy
Our ships passed in Carlsbad
I still don't know why
But friends we became
And friends we are
Ken and I are good buddies
Only now but from afar

Reunion

No fear, no fear, no fear
Only love is welcome here
We will treat each other as brothers
Let peace but draw us near
A unified whole we'll become
Remembering our nature as such
We've always been joined together
We just haven't remembered that much
When we open up to that truth
Of how we all are one
Fear will no longer intercede us
Our reunion will finally be done

Eternal Spring

They come
I write them
This is all I know
They spring from well eternal
The place where all will go
We will gather to quench our thirst there
To taste the one sweet life
That flows from the spring eternal
And washes away all strife
Its gentle waters will cleanse us
Taking away all that is bereft
Of the world we leave to get there
Leaving only innocence left

A Cruel and Guilty Life

I see the guilty you
Brought about by cruel illusion
And that projected on you
For I am that projector
Owner of the guilt for we two
As long as I put it on you
I stay blind to the guilt I choose
This guilt runs a vicious cycle
Back and forth, from me to you
You putting yours on me
And me putting mine on you
There is but one way out
It requires us to stop and choose
Only forgiveness will restore us
To the innocence we both refused
That innocence is our only hope
If we are to stop our strife
It is the only way out
Of this cruel and guilty life

Rejection

My poems have been rejected so much
The tongue in my cheek grows weary
No one wants my jingles
I'm starting to get all teary

Yet I feel for the poor reviewer
Who looks at my repeated pleas
She's likely getting eyes quite bleary
And hoping I stop this, *please*

I'll not give her a break
Or the rest of the world for that matter
I believe they are all worth seeing
They are peace among the clatter

They are gems of truth well hidden
Among rhymes that are out of fashion
I'll not stop til I get you all
To take a look at my compassion

It never ceases to amaze
That truth can go untouched
When everyone in this world
Needs it so very much

Have no fear, my friend
I'll keep writing until I croak
I know there is someone out there
Who waits for a pithy joke

I'll try to wrap one up for you
In all my lyrical rhyme
I'll pose it to you sometime soon
It's bound to be a good ole time

.

Helen & Bill

As my wife's mother's alter ego would say
This was a pair to draw to
The most unlikely duo to write
A most unusual tome of wisdom
A laser beam pointer of light

Intellectuals, scientists, and non-believers
They must have felt not quite right
About scribing this holy manuscript
That would show so many the light

The book did change them
As it has so many of us
Righted their lives and made them
Want to ride this bus

A pre-life contract of sorts
An engagement surely meant
To bring out the best in all of us
And point us Heaven bent

A Mightier Pen

The pen is far mightier than the sword
This I find to be true
Its reach and self evident touch
Can do what no saber can do
One may take a life
One may turn it true
The blade may cut upon us
But can never bring us through
One may only destroy
What the other can turn to life
One so clearly a killer
The other may cease our strife
So lay down your pointer of steel
Pick up the Holy Word
Declare you are no warrior
The best decision ever heard

Gridiron Hero

It's an old football story
Of a gridiron warrior
Beyond his glory

His body was battered and broken
His heart filled with rage
No longer a viable option
To vent his anger uncaged

So he hung up his cleats
On one sad Sunday morn
He said goodbye to his team mates
All but he looked forlorn

For he was still angry
At the body that had let him down
His work, his meaning, his life
Had somehow left town

He sought for a different meaning
Something to make him whole
He found it not in wrestling
Or putting a ball in a hole

He searched somewhat frantically
For something to fill his life
He could not let in his family
His anger shut out his wife

They mourned to see his despair
This man once so proud
He seemed to be so lost now
His desperation spoke so loud

As he wandered from place to place
And then from comfort of love
As he sought the lost meaning
He finally put on the gloves

Now as he entered the arena
And climbed aboard the ring
Facing the fighter before him
It was a pitiful scene
In him, he saw his last chance
He would face another opponent
He would accept this one last dance

The fight was short, not sweet
He barely lasted a round
Before he left his feet
Never to rise again
His life ended in defeat
Leaving a wife and children
A family, now incomplete

She Dances Her Amens

Butterflies danced in her head
Trying to keep pace with her feet
She hardly touched down at all
She had perfected the aerial feat

Known as the loveliest of all
She was the ballerina supreme
As light as air, she was
She could dance a lightening beam

She befuddled a nearby feather
Who couldn't compete or keep up
With the lightest and loveliest ballerina
Whose dance had filled our cup

She finally alit on the floor
We had hoped it would never end
This dance that had been given
Turned out to be her *amen*

Are You

Are you faulty or are you guilty
Are they one in the same
Are you less than you should be
Have you found someone to blame
Are you stuck within your limits
Do you refuse to play
Within those acceptable boundaries
Where you were told to stay
Do you believe in more
Are you willing to let go of less
Can your mind accept the magnificence
Are you willing to be blessed
If you answered in the affirmative
Then there's likely hope for you
There's someone waiting in expectation
To show you what you must do
Accept His grace and blessing
Be amenable to what He says
Merge your will with His

Juiced

Mushroom man, oh mushroom man
Do you have a remedy for dullness
Are your wares available for testing
Are they guaranteed for fullness
Will they replace the liability
That I have grown inside my head
Will they give me peace and guidance
Or grant me visions instead
I think they might have helped a bit
At times when I needed a boost
But they never will replace real love
That's where I get *my* juice

If You Want to See

It is the genius of Christ
This is what I see
Embedded within and between the lines
Available if you want to see

Winners and Losers

Winners and losers
What's this all about
What are we winning and losing
A mini mannequin shout

Is it of real value
To entertain, not its only fee
Is it more than a bread box
Will it set you free

So take your gold medallions
And your glittering statuette too
Compare them to your life
See what they total to

If it pales in contrast to medals
You might want to give it a toss
Try to align your life with
Something that gives no loss

A Lesser Note

He scribed words that lay softly on flowers
The other could tell one helluva joke
One wrapped warm in love words
The other was one kick butt bloke

They have warmed the cockles of my heart
They have rattled the mind box well
Given me a few pointers
Advising I find others to tell

For I have gathered these two souls to me
I am them and they are me
Both, the dearest of brothers
Among the ones we can see

Waldo and George accompanied well
Gave some pause and gave some hell
Gave me a loving sense of humor
And the urge to express it well

I love these two jokers
Jester and poet of note
I sadly do miss them now
The world sings a lesser note

The Oxymoron, the Paradox, and the Contradiction

(The Oxycontradox)

I ran into an oxymoron yesterday
He was lunching with a paradox
They could not agree on a contradiction
They tried, they did
They were, after all, up for discussion
Someone needed to make the call
I'll see if I can get them together
Perhaps some philosophy in the mall
We can debate and talk about it
See if we can figure it out
If not, we'll leave our separate ways
Check out the sales on the way out

Ode to Baby Michael

Twas the day of Michael's birth
And all throughout the house
Not a murmur was intended
No meal for a delinquent mouse

He was just another boy
No legend of the south
He became quite unavoidably
The only one let out

His mother was very happy
His father was quite proud
They welcomed new baby Michael
And heard him say out loud
That he wasn't so happy to be here
He'd rather been left uncrowned

Yet he joined the human race
The one that no one wins
He's planning on doing his best
In the hopes we can all begin
To see what lies before us
The joy behind the veil
To invite and accept the unusual
And wait for sweet love to prevail

Short on Superlatives

I'm short on superlatives
To portray this choice of mine
Far too inadequate to describe
The treasure I did recently find

I really don't know what to call it
It's beyond my ability to say
I suppose it is indescribable
And meant to be that way

All I can say about it
Are these few short words
It's got me all tongue tied
Labeling it seems absurd

You'll just need to take my word for it
You will like it, I am quite sure
Trust me and come silent along
I'll treat you to something pure

Titles Auberge

Do you think me Christ
The receiving hands will know
The fly in my eye just told me
I'm into you for a broken truce
I'm boggled and blown
With no place to stay
I'm the Prince of the Kingdom
From early aplomb, we'll say
The only real sin
Is a medium guy
A place called Home
Is part of the fun
Love in any land
Is a treasure house within
Here as slightly askew
Bearing an ode to a marriage
There's no one to blame
For the direction I go
There's a lesson to be learned from pizza
And a toll to pay for decisions
Which way to pray is the question
Using endless rhyme in prayer
He was there as a stand in
For the Source's non dismal room
The world we bought
With words that touch them true
Only love can say of me
There is no place to start
So I'm going fishin
I have a lovely point of view
Of the race to Christ, my Muse
All those good guys and bad guys

Holding a tighter helm via electrons
Through a shit storm with an old fart
Might need an old fashioned shellacking
Just in case the voodoo we sell
Leaves us as truth remains
Was all he asked of fame
The exquisite friendly flavors
Are better than getting laid
There will be no more boners
Til the ocean's boat denotes
Woof, woof
Christ mine has freed me
From the guilt trip never ending
I'm out the door with this faulty body
Leaving to tune the divine
I'm crazy and loving it
Giving Colorado a second look
The versifier approaches
The Captain of the trumpets
Looking for the same muse
At the nearest unbiased wall
One Mind alone
Made me an entirely new man
Traveling in a foreign land
There's no doubt the new me
Has smaller vices and good posture
I'm on a need to know basis
About friends from afar and the reunion
The eternal spring belies
A cruel and guilty life
Rejection of Helen & Bill
Not the best decision so far
The gridiron hero's wife
Is dancing her amens
Are you juiced and want to see
Winners and losers
Sing a lesser note

The Oxycontradox becomes
An ode to baby Michael
I'm running short of superlatives
To describe the titles at hand

The Need for Doors

The need for doors
And dark hallways
Places to hoard and keep
Those dirty little thoughts
Hiding places for the soul
Just outside the Garden
Keeping us but from our Self
Separate, alone, and undone
The same thought drove us out
Caused belief in life without God
Made a world devoid of love
Keeps us boarded apart
Love requires we leave
The separate thought alone
Come back to the oneness
To where we all belong

Bits

All I want is what I am
All I want is that I am

We are the only ones doing the crucifixion bit

There are no separate interests

I am host to God
And hostage to no one or no thing[1]

1. ACIM—original edition page 301, last line.

Back Where I Was

Not all I have ever said
Has been spoken in love
There is much to regret and deny
I have spoken as broken before
I have blinded love from my eye
I have kept my Father at bay
Nailed shut Heaven's Door
Asked, but never accepted
The most holy of more
What a loss, what a shame
Yet I will regret no more
I have found that long lost to me
Back where I was before

You Sexy Thing

What is it that interests you more
The concave or the convex
Is it shapes and curves
Or is it merely sex
Great boobs and a fine ass
Will get a feel from chiseled chest
Bopping those bongos all night
Giving the sex your best
When it is over and sated
What is left behind
Is it more than love united
Is it a keeper's find
The spur of the moment
The orgasm finally attained
Leaves but with a need
To do it again and again

One of Thee

I am my own biggest fan
I can't help or deny it
I'm amazed at the span
I hope I can find it
For these sweet morsels
Are just as new to me
As they are to you, my friend
I am simply part of thee

Let Love Replace

Brother priest, I feel your pain
My soul prays for your recovery
I know you bear no stain
You are Christ, in truth, my brother
Divine and holy you remain

Yet cease the attack on young brothers
Christ will serve your need
Lust is but the ego
That upon your soul does feed

Deny its intended harm
Let it lessen you no more
Reclaim your divinity, dear priest
Let love replace the whore

Daily Bread

I came into my own
At the top of my sixtieth year
All else was simply preparation
For the last time I would shed a tear

So many miles have led me here
So many bumps along the way
Far too many mistakes
Too much indulgence in the fray

It matters now not at all
It is past and never happened
I come now to install
A ceremony of grand proportions
A step waited long to take
Stepping forth into love's pure welcome
This is something we cannot make

It is born of divine freedom
Woven with joy's tender thread
It is Heaven opened up to us
This is where I make my bed
This is what I choose instead
This becomes my daily bread

Divine Right

I deny my Self no longer
Abundance comes my way
Not a matter of deservement
Not an issue of owed pay
It is simply a divine matter
A gift from God above
A divine right, if you will
It comes in the form of love

No Matter

A miracle of enormous proportion
Has tapped upon my door
Visiting in halls of mind
Never quite seen before

Notifying of Heavenly matters
Gifting from love divine
Bringing me closer to Paradise
Knowing I'll do just fine

All will be well, I'm told
Finally arriving homeward
I've found the pot of gold

It is nothing you'll find here
It doesn't even show up
On the radar that detects the matter
It matters not nor interrupts
The flow of truth in spirit
Or the miracle of the Holy Cup

Captain Emissary

Beloved Holy Spirit
Captain of my ship you are
Your decisions are quite amazing
How could I stray so far

But now I'm back to listen
To hear more of Your refrain
To let Your gentle love guide me
Back to the Holy Main

I could trust you no more
Or less, for that matter
How could I trust my soul
To the hands of any other

Our Father's Emissary, You are
Bringing His Spirit to bear
On a mind and heart so closed
And overcome by fear

Uncertainty has departed
Fear has left the room
Guilt no longer adorns
A mind much better informed
Devoid now of other guidance
Devoid of earthly form

Poet Silenced

Dearest Father, hear my plea
I walk on sacred ground
I do so with impunity
In hope that love will be found

I write that now given
I pray it is written true
For the last thought upon my mind
Is to pay offense to You

Yet I say some things offensive
To the fragile minds of men
Yet never is respect amended
In the future, now, or then

For if I thought I dissed You
I would be forever sad
And ask that you take these hands
And leave me in silence clad

For I could write no more
I would deserve no more the quill
The poet to be silenced
In favor of Thy Holy Will

Paradise Free

I will deceive myself no more
Having fought to be alone
Having crowned a king of my own
Let's face it, I wanted to be alone

Yet fear wears a solitary mask
It hides but the emptiness it is
I have seen the face of loneliness
And seen it to be what it is

My Father offers everything
Forsaken for a run at fame
The truth now assures me
I have traveled the wrong terrain

I see now the choice clearly
Not much of a choice to me
The one course offers nothing
The other is Paradise free

Different Ears

Perhaps you wonder why
My voice does vary so
Between the divine and profane
I will likely let you know
For the Muse has fair intent
He understands you well
He knows that to get to Heaven
May require you recognize hell
He wants you to understand
The trivial is not worth a toss
Divert your attention instead
From the illusion of life and loss
We spend so much time on nothing
When everything is at stake
He wants you to remember
The errant path we did take
So disregard the bullshit
Don't get trapped by the absurd
He speaks to different ears
In words that will be heard